PUG MUGS

OLIVER

COUNTY JAIL
G675 - 9048

PUG MUGS

GOOD PUGS GONE BAD

WILLOW CREEK PRESS

Published by Willow Creek Press
P.O. Box 147, Minocqua, Wisconsin 54548

Photo Credits:
p5 © Hawkes Photography/Liz Kaye Photo Agent; p6 © Jerry Shulman; p9 © Carol Simowitz;
p10 © Daniel Dempster; p13 © Sharon Eide/Elizabeth Flynn;
p14 © Close Encounters of the Furry Kind; p17,18 © Sharon Eide/Elizabeth Flynn;
p21 © John Daniels/Ardea.com; p22 © Cheryl A. Ertelt; p25 © Norvia Behling;
p26 © Sharon Eide/Elizabeth Flynn; p29 © Ron Kimball/ronkimballstock.com;
p30 © Norvia Behling; p33 © Sue Redshaw; p34 © Rosemary Shelton/Click the Photo Connection;
p37 © Jerry Shulman/SuperStock; p38 © Jean M. Fogle; p41 © Ron Kimball/ronkimballstock.com;
p42 © Cris Kelly; p45 © Cheryl A. Ertelt; p46 © Rosemary Shelton/Click the Photo Connection;
p49 © Larry & Marge Grant; p50 © Sharon Eide/Elizabeth Flynn; p53 © Isabelle Francais;
p54 © Rosemary Shelton/Click the Photo Connection; p57; © Jean M. Fogle; p58 © Bonnie Nance;
p61 © Tara Darling; p62 © Norvia Behling; p65 © Jean M. Fogle; p66 © Isabelle Francais;
p69 © Jean M. Fogle; p70 © Norvia Behling; p73 © Isabelle Francais;
p74 © Sharon Eide/Elizabeth Flynn; p77 © Jean M. Fogle;
p78 © Ron Kimball/ronkimballstock.com; p81 © Norvia Behling; p82 © Scott C. Schulman;
p85 © Norvia Behling; p86 © Ron Kimball/ronkimballstock.com; p89,90 © Norvia Behling;
p93 © Sharon Eide/Elizabeth Flynn; p94,96 © Norvia Behling;

Design: Donnie Rubo
Printed in Canada

PUG LOVERS BEWARE:

These dogs are not necessarily the adorable little pooches they appear to be. This book, by way of example and in the spirit of public service, illustrates the nefarious characteristics typically displayed by this peculiar breed. Obtained from canine crime records throughout the land, the following reports represent a laundry list ranging from serious felonies to minor misdemeanors. Be on the lookout for such suspicious pug behavior in and around your residence.

NAME: GIGI
HEIGHT: 11.2"
WEIGHT: 12 LBS.

CHARGE: ATTEMPTED HOMICIDE
Class II felony

Gigi was apprehended in a neighbor's backyard after stalking and attacking a stuffed children's toy. Under questioning it was revealed that the suspect suffers from nearsightedness and was unaware until after the attack that the victim was not, in fact, a live squirrel. Suspect appeared embarrassed yet unrepentant for the incident.

NAME: GONZO
HEIGHT: 9.5"
WEIGHT: 16 LBS.

CHARGE: SHOPLIFTING
Class I misdemeanor

Halted on the street after exiting a local pet store, Gonzo was searched by a store employee. Under his garments were found a rawhide chew stick and two bags of Pupperoni. Suspect was indignant and claimed no knowledge of how the items were found upon his person. Unable to produce a receipt for the goods, and after a loud and belligerent outburst, suspect was transferred to pound.

NAME: WINSTON
HEIGHT: 10.1"
WEIGHT: 11 LBS.

CHARGE: INDECENT EXPOSURE,
URINATING IN PUBLIC
(Third offense)

Class III felony

Winston is a chronic public piddler who has tried and defied his neighborhood's patience and goodwill. Although this is his third arrest, forensic evidence found upon area lawns suggests Winston may be guilty of considerably more transgressions. Should further investigation lead to charges, Winston could be tried as a serial piddler, a Class II felony.

NAME: FINNEGAN
HEIGHT: 10.8"
WEIGHT: 10.5 LBS.

CHARGE: MANSLAUBER

Class III misdemeanor

Finnegan was charged with sneezing and drooling at and upon her master's house guest. After being administered a tissue paper facial, suspect was mildly scolded. When the victim expressed a desire for leniency, charges were dropped and Finnegan was released upon his own recognizance.

NAME: TINA
HEIGHT: 8.8"
WEIGHT: 8.9 LBS.

CHARGE: COERCION AND
FELONIOUS CUTENESS

Class III felony

Tina is a habitual and merciless coercer of hugs and pets from family members, friends and passersby. Her M.O. includes rapidly approaching her target, twirling in rapid circles, then stopping abruptly to greet the victim with an adorable smile. Should this fail to induce a pet, hug or kiss from the victim, Tina will cock her head at a cunning angle certain to produce the desired results.

NAME: OSCAR
HEIGHT: 9.4"
WEIGHT: 13.6 LBS.

CHARGE: PHILANDERING

Class I misdemeanor

Oscar (shown at right in this lineup photograph) has become a neighborhood nuisance and blatant philanderer. Subject is routinely released from house arrest under the pretext of doing his duty only to furtively slip from sight. While his master issues the Come command, Oscar is roaming the neighborhood for winsome females including Yorkies, chihuahuas, dachshunds, and once, incredibly, a Labrador retriever.

PHOTOS NOT ON FILE

CHARGE: GANG BANGING

Class III felony

This litter has in a short time become notorious for riotous behavior and malicious mischief both in and around the home. Criminal allegations include ankle biting, carpet wetting, gnawing on table legs, paper shredding, and general public disturbance. Authorities strongly suggest breaking up the gang after seven weeks and dispersing the pups to new homes where rehabilitation remains a possibility.

NAME: FELIX
HEIGHT: 12"
WEIGHT: 12.7 LBS.

CHARGE: NONSUPPORT AND
FAMILY NEGLECT

Class I misdemeanor

DNA evidence confirms that Felix is the sire of a litter of 12-week-old pups yet subject ignores all responsibility and claims no knowledge of how the puppies showed up in the first place. He appears at times bewildered by their presence. As for the mother of the litter, Felix has shown no interest since their brief, romantic tryst.

NAME: PEPPY
HEIGHT: 9"
WEIGHT: 8.8 LBS.

CHARGE: TAMPERING WITH/DESTROYING FEDERAL PROPERTY

Class II felony

Although a known felon, Peppy has nonetheless gained the grudging respect of authorities for his skill and audacity. Aided by extraordinary canine cunning, Peppy not only deduces the delivery of United States mail originating from the local veterinarian, he additionally scales the pole, opens the door of the mailbox, and chews the vet's letters. By such device has Peppy managed to avoid his rabies shots for the past two years.

NAME: BRANDO
HEIGHT: 14"
WEIGHT: 11.4 LBS.

CHARGE: REBELLIOUS WITHOUT A CAUSE
Class III misdemeanor

Brando's recent arrest for rebellious behavior only adds to an already lengthy rap sheet that includes refusal to come when called, fighting with other dogs, and miscellaneous general disturbances. When asked what exactly he is rebelling against, Brando was purported to utter, "Whaddaya got?" Suspect is considered incorrigible.

NAME: MILLY
HEIGHT: 9"
WEIGHT: 10 LBS.

CHARGE: FAILURE TO SHARE

Class III misdemeanor

Milly and Pete are two Pugs residing together at 712 E. Beaumont Avenue. Complaint indicates that Milly will no longer allow cohabitation of that comfy overstuffed green chair in the den and has repeatedly threatened plaintiff with low growls and bared teeth upon his approach to said chair. Authorities suggest temporary separation and counseling.

NAME: BONGO
HEIGHT: 13"
WEIGHT: 10.5 LBS.

CHARGE: POSSESSION OF DRUG PARAPHERNALIA

Class I misdemeanor

The occupants of a local residence suspected of drug traf-
ficking were apparently tipped off in advance of a recent
raid by authorities. An extensive search of the residence
turned up drug paraphernalia and a lone Pug whose collar
identified him as "Bongo." The dog, apparently left behind
by the suspects in their hasty departure, appeared unfazed,
even mellow, despite the rush of police activity.

NAME: MAX
HEIGHT: 10"
WEIGHT: 12 LBS.

CHARGE: MAKING CRANK PHONE CALLS
Class II misdemeanor

A continuing investigation into suspicious calls originating from 322 Elm St. has left authorities perplexed to date. The married tenants both work regular hours and have no children at home. Nevertheless, for the past several weeks, daily, between the hours of 9 a.m. and 5 p.m., several local pizzeria and Chinese restaurants complain of receiving food orders originating from the phone number corresponding to that address. No one is present to accept delivery of these orders and only a faint scratching is heard behind the door.

NAME: OTTO
HEIGHT: 12"
WEIGHT: 13.2 LBS.

CHARGE: OBSTINANCE

Class II misdemeanor

Following a string of incidences during which he was difficult to manage and control, Otto was reported to authorities. "He simply refuses to come when he's called," stated owner Nancy Ferguson in her complaint. "He just stands there and stares with a 'Make me' kind of look on his face." As a result of the incident, Otto has been fitted with a leash and will be monitored, and his outdoor activities will be closely supervised.

NAME: PENNY
HEIGHT: 11"
WEIGHT: 11.7 LBS.

CHARGE: STOLEN MOTOR VEHICLE
Class I felony

The cause of a recent rash of stolen toy vehicles belonging to Jack Jones, six-year-old son of Don and Patti Jones, has recently been solved. Using motion-activated photo technology, authorities caught Penny exiting the playroom with a monster truck firmly secured in her jaws. After a hot pursuit at speeds reaching four miles per hour, Penny was cornered in the basement where seven other missing vehicles were also found.

PHOTOS NOT ON FILE

CHARGE: VOYEURISM

Class I felony

Chester and Tucker are two male Pugs residing at 303 Lexington Street. Authorities have received repeated calls from the next door neighbor complaining that the dogs habitually linger at their dining room window during the dinner hour and closely watch while the family eats. "They follow every single bite from the plate to our mouth, and they don't leave until the table's cleared," states the neighbor. An investigation into the complaint continues at this time.

NAME: ANNIE
HEIGHT: 13"
WEIGHT: 12.6 LBS.

CHARGE: LEAVING THE SCENE OF AN ACCIDENT

Class II misdemeanor

Eyewitness reports allege that Annie, an unleashed Pug on a public beach, urinated several times in the presence of onlookers before wandering off. Later apprehended at a nearby concession stand, she was returned to her owners without further incident.

NAME: PHOEBE
HEIGHT: 11"
WEIGHT: 9.8 LBS.

CHARGE: CONTRIBUTING TO THE DELINQUENCY OF A MINOR

Class I misdemeanor

Phoebe is a six-year-old Pug and mother of 12-week-old Daisy. Although Phoebe is fully trained and understands that the furniture in the living room is strictly off limits, she has nonetheless been frequently observed lying on the sofa. To compound this illegal behavior, she now encourages Daisy to join her in these crimes. Authorities recommend withholding treats for one week.

NAME: TANYA
HEIGHT: 14"
WEIGHT: 13 LBS.

CHARGE: PUBLIC NUISANCE/PANHANDLING
Class III misdemeanor

Roaming without a leash in a public park, Tanya was observed approaching passersby and aggressively begging for handouts. She had disappeared by the time authorities responded to complaints. The incident remains under investigation.

NAME: ROSEY
HEIGHT: 13"
WEIGHT: 10.9 LBS.

CHARGE: SOLICITING

Class I misdemeanor

Rosey is a four-year-old Pug currently in heat. Complaints site that Rosey has recently been trolling the neighborhood in search of likely suitors, sometimes boldly appearing at the doorsteps of homes of local male dogs. She has since been apprehended and sentenced to two weeks of home confinement.

NAME: QUINCY
HEIGHT: 8"
WEIGHT: 6.7 LBS.

CHARGE: JUVENILE DELINQUENCY
Class III misdemeanor

The Anderson household has been subjected to a series of chewing incidents associated with Quincy, an 11-week-old teething Pug. "If he can fit it in his mouth, he'll chew it," states Mrs. Anderson in her complaint. Probation has been granted on the condition Quincy confines his chewing to rawhide sticks.

NAME: FRANCIS
HEIGHT: 11"
WEIGHT: 9.3 LBS.

CHARGE: BALL HOG
Class III misdemeanor

Francis is a habitual ball hog who obstructs the play of both his littermates and the children in his household. His reluctance to share has led to home confinement with future charges pending.

NAME: BURT
HEIGHT: 14"
WEIGHT: 12.5 LBS.

CHARGE: PUBLIC NUISANCE/DISTURBING THE PEACE

Class III misdemeanor

Responding to complaints of excessive neighborhood noise, authorities found Burt howling and baying in his backyard. A further investigation noted that the dog was responding painfully to the sounds of a Kenny G CD emanating from a nearby home. Burt was praised and released without further action.

PHOTOS NOT
ON FILE

CHARGE: ATTEMPTED ESCAPE

Class I misdemeanor

Duke and Jack are two Pugs with a known record for leaving the yard. Temporarily incarcerated in an outside pen for the benefit of fresh air, the suspects burrowed beneath, pushed against, and climbed the bars in continued attempts to escape. Exasperated officials returned them to home confinement where charges are pending.

NAME: SADIE
HEIGHT: 13"
WEIGHT: 12.3 LBS.

CHARGE: UNCOOPERATIVE BEHAVIOR
Class III misdemeanor

Apparently morose at being left behind at the local
kennel while the rest of the family visits Six Flags
Amusement Park over the weekend, security guards
described Sadie as listless, without appetite, and
generally uncooperative. Authorities recommend release
from solitary confinement on Monday morning.

NAME: CARLO
HEIGHT: 11"
WEIGHT: 9.4 LBS.

CHARGE: WILLFUL DISOBEDIENCE
Class III misdemeanor

Although semi-house trained, Carlo was placed behind bars when the seven-week-old Pug piddled on the living room rug three times during the course of a two hour period. Carlo was so overjoyed upon his release one-half hour later that he immediately peed in the kitchen.

CHARGE: INDOLENCE

Class III misdemeanor

A litter of two-week old Pugs owned by Matt and
Tamra Consie reportedly sleep up to 12 hours daily,
greatly disappointing the Consie's six-year-old
daughter, Lauren, who wishes to play with them. The
pups have been given a three week probation after
which it is expected their activity level will delight
Lauren and overwhelm her parents.

NAME: MAURICE
HEIGHT: 15"
WEIGHT: 16.7 LBS.

CHARGE: LEWD & LASCIVIOUS BEHAVIOR
Class III misdemeanor

Maurice, age eleven years, is described by some witnesses as "a dirty old Pug"; by others as "an incurable romantic." In either light and despite his advanced age, Maurice chronically approaches female dogs of all breeds in assertive attempts to mate. Although continually rebuffed, Maurice remains shamelessly persistent, or as one local official observed, "That dog can still hunt."

NAME: REGGIE
HEIGHT: 13"
WEIGHT: 12.1 LBS.

CHARGE: STALKING
Class III misdemeanor

Reggie is currently under questioning by authorities after numerous complaints from guests attending a barbecue in the backyard of Keith and Helen Henderson stating that the four-year-old Pug continually approached and lingered around the diners in a suspicious manner. "He'd just stand there looking at you, hoping for something to fall off your plate," stated one witness. "It was just plain eerie."

NAME: KIKI
HEIGHT: 11"
WEIGHT: 10.6 LBS.

CHARGE: IMPERSONATING AN OFFICER

Class II felony

Kiki's false identity as a security officer was sniffed out at a public beach last Saturday by two Labrador retrievers. Authorities dropped charges after determining that Kiki had "suffered enough" through sheer embarrassment.

NAME: TEENCEE
HEIGHT: 13"
WEIGHT: 12.3 LBS.

**CHARGE: PUBLIC NUISANCE/
OFFENSIVE ODOR**

Class III misdemeanor

After being observed rolling in foul smelling fecal mat-
ter of unknown origin in the backyard, Teencee was
immediately apprehended and sentenced to a bath. A judge
later ruled that the punishment did not fit the crime
given the extent of the lingering odor. As a result, her
sentence was extended to one night in the family garage.

NAME: RUSTY
HEIGHT: 14"
WEIGHT: 13.9 LBS.

CHARGE: ENDANGERING PERSONAL SAFETY

Class III misdemeanor

A poor swimmer, Rusty nonetheless, last Sunday, attempted to paddle across the full-length of the family pool in an apparent attempt to impress a female Yorkie visiting that afternoon. Rusty was rescued after floundering, sputtering and snorting mid-way through his foolhardy attempt. Suspect was toweled off and no further action was taken.

NAME: ABBIE
HEIGHT: 12"
WEIGHT: 10 LBS.

CHARGE: ACCEPTING A BRIBE

Class III misdemeanor

Disinclined to ingest her pills by legal means, Abbie induced her owner to bribery using peanut butter as the payoff. The suspect has been under surveillance for weeks and authorities are convinced they have an open and shut case.

NAME: BAILEY
HEIGHT: 13"
WEIGHT: 12.8 LBS.

CHARGE: BREAKING AND EXITING

Class III misdemeanor

A bold sleuth and expert lock pick, Bailey has developed the expertise to open his kennel cage and roam at will before re-entering and locking himself in once again. This illegal activity remains unknown to his owners who are puzzled by the continuing disappearance of food items placed on the lowest refrigerator shelf.

NAME: TAKEELA
HEIGHT: 17"
WEIGHT: 19.2 LBS.

CHARGE: DAMAGE TO A MOTOR VEHICLE
Class III misdemeanor

The crime scene is the interior of a 1961 Austin Healey 3000. The challenge to authorities: two Pugs, one wet spot. After lengthy questioning, Takeela, shown at left, finally broke and admitted to the crime.

NAME: CATO
HEIGHT: 12"
WEIGHT: 9.7 LBS.

CHARGE: INTIMIDATION
Class III misdemeanor

His diminutive size notwithstanding, Cato is a ferocious defender of the front gate of his home — so much so that uniformed representatives of the U.S. Postal Service have advised his owners that mail delivery will be halted unless action is taken. As a result, Cato has been relieved from further duty and is reassigned to security issues within the household.

NAME: HARLEY
HEIGHT: 14"
WEIGHT: 12.7 LBS.

CHARGE: PUBLIC NUISANCE/PEEPING TOM
Class III misdemeanor

Authorities responding to a neighborhood complaint of a peeping Tom observed a three-year-old Pug identified as Harley staring at them from a nearby picket fence. "Downright unnerving" one official was reported as saying. Suspect fled as authorities approached and a house to house search is underway

NAME: DOLLY
HEIGHT: 16"
WEIGHT: 14.2 LBS.

CHARGE: PETTY THEFT
Class III misdemeanor

The facts in this case are clear: there are two plastic chew bones in the Adams' household, one for Dolly; one for Coco. Not satisfied with this arrangement, Dolly hides her bone and swipes Coco's acting as if it were her own. A search of the household for evidence of Dolly's bone is underway before charges can be filed.

NAME: PUCK
HEIGHT: 13"
WEIGHT: 11.8 LBS.

CHARGE: FUGITIVE FLIGHT
Class III misdemeanor

While secured and being escorted by a leash from his household to the public park, Puck broke from his master and fled for two hundred yards and was found hiding in a lilac bush. The dog gave up passively and the walk continued without further incident.

NAME: WILLIE
HEIGHT: 11"
WEIGHT: 10.2 LBS.

CHARGE: FRAUD
Class III misdemeanor

An examination by a local veterinarian has determined that Willie, who has repeatedly failed to come when called, is not deaf after all. Armed with this new evidence, prosecutors will vigorously pursue a sentence of life-on-a-leash.

NAME: ANGEL
HEIGHT: 15"
WEIGHT: 13.7 LBS.

CHARGE: MALICIOUS MISCHIEF
Class III misdemeanor

The suspicious behavior of Angel, a 10-year-old pug known to lurk around neighborhood trampolines, led authorities to search his residence where a collection of well-chewed tennis shoes was found in the bedroom closet. Angel, aka one-eyed-lefty, was taken into custody without incidence, and when questioned, offered no explanation for why all of the shoes were for the right foot only.

NAME: MICKEY
HEIGHT: 13"
WEIGHT: 11.9 LBS.

CHARGE: SOLICITING

Class III misdemeanor

Mickey, a three-year-old pug on weekend shore leave, was apprehended during a police sting operation involving an undercover female poodle. While authorities allege that Mickey was soliciting the officer, Mickey maintains his innocence and claims he was merely asking for directions back to the dock.

NAME: LESTER
HEIGHT: 14"
WEIGHT: 13.5 LBS.

CHARGE: PUBLIC INTOXICATION
Class III misdemeanor

Lester, unaware that the liquid spilled on the kitchen tile was a vodka martini, licked every last drop before embarrassing himself at his master's dinner party. Several incidents of misbehavior, including upsetting the appetizer platter and jumping on laps, were reported by guests. Lester was sentenced to a St. Bernard-sized hangover.

NAME: QUINN
HEIGHT: 15"
WEIGHT: 14.3 LBS.

CHARGE: DISORDERLY CONDUCT
Class III misdemeanor

Awakened by a scuffle on their front porch, Paul and Kate Cook of St. Croix, Minnesota, were appalled to witness Quinn, their five-year-old pug, in the middle of a brawl with two neighborhood cats. The ruckus was loud enough to alert an area patrolman, who determined the fight was over the dominion of the porch. Although Quinn suffered a scratched nose and a torn collar, he remained belligerent and insistent that "no cat" is a threat to him. His status as "Big Dog" on the porch is now in question.

NAME: TINA
HEIGHT: 12"
WEIGHT: 11.2 LBS.

CHARGE: UNBEARABLE HAUGHTINESS
Class III misdemeanor

Tina's personal history was that of a well-behaved and friendly Pug. Since being fitted with a jewel-encrusted collar, however, her attitude has allegedly changed markedly. "She's acting like a snotty little princess," claims owner Marjorie Simpson.